CITY LINES

Poems by London School Students

CITY LINES

Poems by London School Students

ILEA English Centre

Copyright © 1982 with individual authors
Compiled and designed by Michael Simons, Mike Raleigh and
Paul Ashton
Competition organiser and editor: Paul Ashton
Typeset by Kate Haggart
Printed and bound by A. Wheaton, Exeter and London
Front cover: mural by Greenwich Mural Workshop
Front cover. photograph: Michael Simons
Published by ILEA English Centre, Sutherland Street,
London SW1.
The English Centre is a teachers' centre for English teachers
within the Inner London Education Authority.
ISBN   0 907016 022 2

The judges of the English Centre Poetry Competition 1981
were Andrew Bethell, Zoe Fairbairns, Archie Markham, John
Richmond and Mike Rosen.

CONTENTS

INTRODUCTION

The English Centre Poetry Competition held in 1981
attracted many thousands of entries. The poems in
this collection from ILEA schools show something of
the enormous range of styles and subjects, from bombs
to beaches, from guitars to grandmothers.

The school students who wrote these poems clearly
felt that, whether their subject was jokey or serious,
about things inside their heads or out in the world,
poetry was a good way of sharing their ideas with other
people.

Sometimes we've included comments from the authors
which help to explain how they came to write their
poems. The photographs have been chosen to capture
the spirit of some of the poems; they are not meant to
be exact illustrations.

Who is That Woman?

Who is that woman?
Don't know.
Well, I heard she lives
down the street. And
she just moved in, she
looks kind of friendly,
but I don't know. Somehow
her face seems quite natural,
but I don't know.
She smiles, if you smile,
she smiles at the sun,
and runs up and down
the street, energetically.
She is so sympathetic,
asking no questions,
demanding nothing of us.
But I don't know.
I heard she comes from Cyprus,
and does not speak our language.
She wanders sadly home,
looks back,
but there is no-one to be seen.
She listens,
trying to catch a few words.
Silently, silently
the door shuts.
I don't know.

Sonia Vigo

How I came to write this poem was from a childhood memory I used to have. I remembered the woman very clearly; she lived in my village in Spain. I thought she was lonely, and at times I felt sorry for her. Rumours went round the village she was mad, and that she came from another planet. Of course that was nonsense and childish. But the men in my village really believed this, and the women as well. The children used to tease her a lot. But she tried to make friends with them. I remember that woman so well, that she will always stay in my mind as a special woman. She could cope with loneliness, and she could understand what was happening. But she was not mad, she was just unhappy, because I think she was not loved by anyone.

A Stranger

In a foreign country
I wriggle from sorrow
As I don't know
Where to go,
Where to stand.
I feel so lonely,
I feel so strange
My steps are hesitant
Along the foreign land
As I walk.
        People around me
Are talking happily
But they talk different

a different place
a different language

and I am in between.

Katerina Theoharous

A Letter to Jo in Jamaica

The wind blows sweetly
in long summer days
you tell me and involve me.

Colourful fish come
from the boats on
the sea shore, every day.

I wake up in dark
and misty mornings
half the year.

You have sunshine, sunshine,
the flame tree echoing
and the nightingale.

You eat food
with sugar and spices.
I eat mashed potatoes.

I stand in heavy clothes
against my skin.
You go about light, golden brown
like polished mahogany.

Joan Davidson

Yesterday, Today, Tomorrow

Yesterday I was younger,
Yesterday I believed
That God watched over the world at large,
That real dairy butter was better than marg,
That the good guys were good and the bad guys were bad,
That no-one in power could really be mad
That a friend in need was a friend indeed,
That only women bleed.

But today I've seen it all, and now I know better.

Today I am
anti-rich and anti-poor
anti-you lot having more,
anti-pigeons, anti-cars,
anti-shuttle-trips to Mars,
anti-nuclear power,
anti-news on the hour,
anti-Thatcher, anti-Reagan
anti-Hitler, anti-Begin,
anti-'O'-levels and CSE's,
anti-intellectuals with Economy degrees,
anti-yellow phoneboxes, and red ones, too,
anti-paying in public loos,
anti-drink and anti-drugs,
anti-Charles and Diana mugs,
But tomorrow . . .

Tomorrow I'll give up,
I won't try to change the world,
I will realise, acknowledge and accept.
I won't show surprise when the leader I'm following lies
And I won't know how to reject.
Tomorrow I'll watch telly while I'm eating my lunch,
And if they show a little violence — who cares?
I'll be a Conservative but think I'm a radical,
I'll sit back and enjoy the decline,
I'll shop at Safeways or Tescos or Spar,
Rip up yours to make mine.
Tomorrow the apathy sets in,
And I'll welcome it, sit back and grin,
I'll paint my toenails with Mary Quant,
I'll do whatever they think I want.

Maureen Miles

I Thought a Lot of You

I thought you were my friend,
I thought you said you'd help;
I thought I could trust you,
I thought I could count on you;
I thought you were loyal,
I thought you would understand;
I thought I made it sound straight-forward,
I thought I had someone to talk to;
I thought you had an answer,
I thought you were a good listener;
I thought I was telling in confidence,
I thought I wasn't being stupid;
I thought you wouldn't make a fool of me,
I thought you weren't going to tell a soul;
    I thought wrong!

P.S. Blackman (Jnr.)

My First Language

My first language:
A relief, comfortable secret
Helping me, hindering me,
Making me a stranger.

My second language:
Powerful

Two strange languages inside my head.

Juan Berganinos Fuentes

Mentally Handicapped

Walking
with mother,
Like it always does,
Wading through the rainy weather
It always looks for us.

Running
Towards us,
Hoping to play,
Hands wagging lifelessly,
A sign to run away.

Staring
From the steamed up window.
"Is HE looking at us?"
Eyes that never meet eyes,
Looking from the bus.

Danny Cerqueira

It was an extra hot day and no-one wanted to do any work, let alone write poetry, the most dreaded English topic. However it was impossible to get out of it. As it was the International Year of the Disabled the poems were to be on the theme of the disabled. At first, like everyone else in the class I was very reluctant to do it but as I said there was no getting out of it. I tried to go about it in a methodical way and thought carefully about what to write.
The whole poem was taken from memories of when I was about nine years old. A mongol boy lived across the road from me. I never used to play with him because he was different and I was afraid of that. Whenever he saw me he'd shout out, 'What's your name, boy?' Although I always used to tell him, he'd ask me the same question the next time he saw me. I now realise that his mother must have been the most patient of people. I dedicated the first verse to her

*because she devoted herself to him and even walked
out in the rain with him to keep him happy. His
mother was the one I always saw him with and she
was his best friend.*

*While thinking of that boy (I never learnt his name)
I remembered a mentally handicapped girl. Although
I never saw her as often as the boy I did learn her
name. Her name was Naomi and about six years ago
she was twenty two years old and very much depend-
ent on her mother. The second verse is dedicated to
Naomi.*

*It was one day in particular which inspired me to
write the second verse. I was with a couple of friends
and we were waiting for their mother. We were laughing and having fun when Naomi saw us. Obviously
she wanted join in the fun and ran ahead of her
mother towards us. Her hands wagged when she ran.
We heard a voice, 'Quick, get away from there.' I was
ready to run before I heard the voice and ran across
the road rapidly without thinking about cars. My
friends and I took the incident with nervous excite-
ment. I felt terribly guilty afterwards but I didn't tell
anyone of my guilt lest my friends laughed at me.*

*This brings me to the shape of the poem. I isolated
the words at the beginning of each verse to show that
mentally handicapped people do like to do what any
other person does. I wrote the HE in the third verse
in block capitals to show that mentally handicapped
people have their own personalities. They are a he or
a she not an IT. Many people exaggerate greatly when
they pretend not to know whether a mongol is a boy
or a girl. I made the other lines shorter to make the
poem look more interesting.*

*Finally the last verse was again referring to a particular
day: while I was waiting for the bus to go to school,
the familiar blue bus stopped in the traffic. The other
people at the bus stop pretended not to see the children
lolling up and down in the bus. I saw the boy of whom
I write inside. His dull eyes were staring out of his
hanging head. He was breathing onto the window so
that it steamed up and hid his face. That memory was
the first thing I remembered when writing the poem
and I doubt that it is one that I shall ever forget.*

Ice Palace

Palaces made out of minds,
Living, breathing, giving thought.
Ticking over, making lives,
Their conceptions can't be bought.

Minds are made of different things,
Compounds, elements, ideas,
Sensitive to roots in air,
Fingertips and eyes and ears.

Some are built of solid stone,
Sensible and good and strong.
They can stand the heavy load,
Can endure, however long.

Other minds are made of buds,
Fragrant roses, soft and pure.
They are young and love to live,
Full of truths but never sure.

Some are castles built of ice,
Pinnacles that never melt,
Empty caverns, lonely, dark,
Full of feelings never felt.

When the rosebud meets the ice
Lovely petals surely freeze.
Starved of warmth, they fade and die,
Wept for by the lonely breeze.

Petals need a home of stone,
Something safe and bright and warm,
Someone strong and good and sure
To protect them from the storm.

Roses must beware of love,
However much it may entice.
They must know their lover's mind,
Else they perish in the ice.

Angela C. Payne

Final Scene

Think in terms of bridges burned,
Think of seasons that must end,
See the rivers rise and fall,
They will rise and fall again.
Everything must have an end,
Like an ocean to a shore,
Like a river to a stream,
It's the famous FINAL SCENE.

Now the lines have all been read,
And you know them off by heart,
Now you walk towards the door,
Here it comes, the hardest part.
Try the handle of the road,
Feeling different, feeling strange,
This can never be arranged,
As the light fades from the screen,
It's the famous FINAL SCENE.

Kathleen Edwards

The Kiss

On my skirt
I had the book opened.
His black curls lay on my cheek.

Neither of us saw the words
I think
But instead kept
A deep silence.
How long it lasted?
Not even then I knew.

I only know that
Only our breath could be heard
Which pressurized escape
Over the dry lip.

I only know
That we both turned at the one time,
Our eyes met
And we kissed.

Delia Perez

Lies

He said he would bring
flowers, but never said
when

He said my eyes were nice
but never said beautiful

He said he would hold my
hands, but never did

He said he would kiss me but
only did when he said good-
bye, and that was on my hands

Virginia Fletcher

The Wastes of Time

On the mantlepiece stands the clock
that has been with me
since my thirtieth year.
I once took no notice of it,
but now sitting alone
in this silent, silent house
I realise that
with its unrelenting cold hand
that clock is marking carefully
my last years;
puncturing the days with its strike
and fracturing the hours.
What has an old man to do
but sit alone and listen to the clock
and wonder that such a simple,
unfeeling object
should be appointed to tell him
how slowly fast
his time is running out?

When you sit alone
and are old
your thoughts speed like lean whippets
shouted on over the heath,
finding a target at any point
of your life's memories.
Making you remember with their probing muzzles
mourned youth.
And I was once young.
I can remember that.
Then movement came as easily
as water flowing down stream.
Thoughts were of the moment,
of now,
not death, not tomorrow death.
Death because I am old.

A stick, white hair, dim eyes,
old, declining,
down, down to the endless pit of eternity.
Old, always thought of as old,
an old man . . .
I lie alone in bed at night
and out of the darkness
I can see a child eager-eyed.
I can see a youth kissing a girl.
I can see a man,
strong and upright,
a man, a man.
And I know that was me
but the clock on the mantlepiece
makes it hard to remember
what it was like . . .

Denise King

*I suppose this poem was written out of a feeling of
how awful it must be to be at the end of one's life and
look back at the passing of that very precious possess-
ion, youth. Of course old age can't be entirely a matter
of regret and sadness but I dare say that for a number
of the old loneliness and fear overshadow a fair prop-
ortion of their lives. Perhaps since I was seventeen
when I wrote it you could say that the poem reflects
as well the young's fear of age.*
*The poem does concentrate on the physical losses
entailed in getting old apart from just the loneliness
aspect. I imagine the subject to have been a working
man with a physical type of job, so therefore he would
feel more keenly the loss of sheer physical capacity
than, say, someone with a sedentary job.*

Maybe a Cherry Sunburst

Maybe a cherry sunburst or plain, natural,
But mine is black.

Sits on my thigh, inviting.
Scratch the hard steel and
She'll sing you a song.

From a million miseries come forth
Her haunting beauty.
Many times a good-time girl,
Though not like you're thinking.
Never like that,
For she's very dignified.

No, a foot-stompin', hand-clappin' style,
That's her.
She'll make you laugh and sing!

She can be temperamental, mind.
Many's the time she's scorned and screamed,
Cursing my careless fingers.
It doesn't matter, though.
She forgives me and I feel ashamed
Of what I did.

Forever under your spell,
My six-stringed blues-gal.

Andrew Richmond

Wishes, Lies, Dreams, Fears

Frustrated teenager, cradling a wish,
Holding tight to it as days and weeks pass,
Thinking of it, always changing.
Help! my life needs rearranging.
I want to go to Germany: a fish
Out of water I feel, at home and in class.

"Oh yes, my 'A' levels," I say gaily
To friends, teachers, parents; I pretend there's nothing
wrong.
"History, English, Music," I know I'm lying
Cursing my cowardice and sighing.
— I tried once, I remind myself daily;
My mind won't concentrate — in self-defence — for long.

Ich traume . . . Wohnen mit Vater und
Zwei Halbschwester, Schule schaff' ich.
Seit Weinachten werd' ich van Gewissen gezerrt
Nach England, nach Deutschland, in mein Zimmer gesperrt:
"Kann ich so verlieren-Bruder, Mutter, Kater,
Freundn — weh tun kann ich sie? Affig!"

I fear my mother's reaction, she'll be offended —
Sad? I think so but hope not; in January I told her
I'd rather stay in Germany, I'm insecure at home,
Don't fit in school, never have, I'm alone —
Can I tell her again? Can mistrust be mended
or, if I stay, will resentment smoulder?

(translation of verse three:
I dream . . . living with father and
Two half-sisters, I'll manage school.
Since Christmas I'm pulled about by my conscience
To England, to Germany, locked in my room:
"Can I lose them — brother, mother, cat,
Friend — can I hurt them? Stupid!)

Ruth Tuschling

PART OF THE FAMILY

The Beach

The agony and turmoil
of when family meet beach!
Argument of where to pitch
Of when to eat
Of what to play
Sand-infested lunches
Tar on every towel
Car boots full of festering sea shells
And claws of crabs and wood.
Parents sprawled while children pester
Hourly marches to the loos
Stones that cripple
Freezing water
Punctured air beds and broken flip-flops
High tide at mid-day
Itchy sandy walks back to the oven-like car
Bad tempered traffic-jams
Arguments as to which turning to go down
    No telly in the evening
    — boring game of cards.

Sarah Wilson

Don't Interrupt!

Turn the television down!
None of your cheek!
Sit down!
Shut up!
Don't make a fool of yourself!
Respect your elders!
I can't put up with you anymore!
Go outside.
Don't walk so fast!
Don't run.
Don't forget to brush your teeth!
Don't forget to polish your shoes!
Don't slam the door!
Have manners!
Don't interrupt when I'm talking!
Put your hand over your mouth when you cough.
Don't talk with your mouth full!
Go to the market with me.
You spend too much money!
No more pocket money for you dear.
Go to your room!
Don't stuff yourself with sweets!
Don't point!
Don't go too near the television.
You are not coming out until you have tidied your room.
Don't interrupt when I'm talking!
Did you get any homework today?
Always carry a pen to school.
Eat your dinner up.
Wear your school uniform!
Turn the television over to watch 'Dallas'.
Bring any letters home from school.
Come straight home tomorrow.
Tidy your bed.
Don't shout!
Don't listen to my conversation.
Don't look at the sun it could blind you.
Don't bite your nails!
Don't suck your thumb!
Why don't you answer me!
You never listen to a word I say!
Don't interrupt when I'm talking!

Demetroulla Vassili

Reflecting

Deflating like a Michelin man,
my mother's home-truths acting
as a penknife-ripping ego.
Reflecting, the mirror tells no lies —
the body like a topless pear,
hips ready for virgin childbirth,
an hourglass with no link
between the hours.
Cheeks with the fat
of a thousand babies, non-existent
cheekbones, the suggestion
of a moustache
(the curse of every beauty queen).
Perched on a small plum,
the glasses thick enough
to enlarge the pupils, bulge the eyes.

The home-truths hitting home.

Jennifer Mitchell

The Family

She arrives home with a problem,
Needing time to think.
Mother and father, grey and old,
Kiss her.
She walks in,
Expensive clothes
Strong odour of French perfume
Whilst the parents cling to their drab grey world
And the tired apartment.
The parents, grateful for the time she's given them,
Forget when all their time was hers,
No appreciation for their used-up bodies
Given away for her.
She may realise there is no reason to feel guilty,
But she just doesn't have the time.
The people who gave her all their time and energy
Have become a butt for her jokes.
She meant to phone, but . . .
Or write, only . . .
But anyhow, she's home now,
So what's the difference?
They're only her parents
But she outgrew them long ago;
She outgrew them,
So why does she need to make excuses?
Because she loves them,
and after all, they are her parents . . .

Jenny Fromer

Sixteen

Alone, on a train
With the pouring rain
Matching your tears.
The train wheels sing out,
Never come back, never come back, never come back . . .

Had a row with your parents,
Their opinions and ideas,
Don'ts and do's
Still the wheels sing out,
Never come back, never come back, never come back.

Jeanette Sharp

Grandmother

She's dead.
The words put a sudden stop to one of my inner thoughts
And already new thoughts planted themselves
And started growing.
A part of me wanted to yell out and ask for my
                                        Grandmother back.
But ask who?
What right had I? I was only an intruder.
That fact of life caused the most pain,
A secret pain that no one will ever seek out its hiding
                                                    place.
Was this my part for mourning?
My father, the son,
My mother, the daughter-in-law,
And me. Which character did I play?
I had passed her life as a complete stranger.
And I blame time for this.
For my Grandmother, time was long enough.
For me, it was too short.

Sonia Pearce

*I wrote this poem a few weeks after my grandmother
died. It was written through anger, an anger that I can
only express through writing. The fact was that my
Mum and I were planning to go and see her at the end
of the year. During the time I used to wonder, would
I ever get to Jamaica to see her? What did she look
like? Would I like her?*

*Then I heard she was dead. Suddenly my thoughts
were forced to change, and I began thinking, would
we be able to go for the funeral? Would it be worth
going? Through this I got angry, not at anyone, but by
the way it had to end. The shape of my poem is a
reflection to show what I was thinking.*

*My grandmother knew my father, and my mother, and
she met my sister, but though she played a part in my
life, we never got to know each other, not even through
letters. We were strangers, and that was what hurt the
most. I got confused over whether to miss her or not,
because in one way her death could have affected me
as little as the death of a stranger in the street. Your
feelings are decided by how much you know the
person.*

*And so I blame time for it. My grandmother died at
the age of 99, and I was 16 when it happened. It
seemed that my grandmother had been waiting a long
time to see me, much longer than I waited to see her,
but we didn't overlap enough to make it possible. And
so because of time we will always remain strangers.*

gone

he is
and six feet deep

there are those who will
shuffle around in upstairs rooms
push half-eaten sandwiches under the breakfast table
whisper half-remembered truths
to those that know them better

i never knew him
but neither did you
the crow is calling in the bitter wind
while you hang dead around
his broken neck

still, he is gone
and finished with all this.

Martin Murphy

The Funeral of Father

Black,
They all wore black.
Even the cat wore black.

Flowers.
Wreaths of flowers.
Gardens of flowers
for him who only grew vegetables.
Mother.
Mother wept
forgetting the black eyes he gave her.
And brother,
my brother didn't care
to remember the beatings.
Only I spat on the coffin
as it dropped
and said something
my sister wouldn't tell the vicar,
who, while reading the service,
scratched his nose.
And that was the end of Father.

Back home we drank
the sherry from under the stairs.
Aunt Flo remembered early years
when Father was a lad.
I smiled,
infamous by now
for my lack of gravity.
I smiled and said aloud,
"He was the biggest bastard
you ever knew,"
and then,
as the clock passed one,
they had an honest moment;
but nobody denounced
the prodigal son
with his two-tone shoes.
That was the memory of Father.

Denise King

39

Me and My Family

My mum is on a diet,
　　My dad is on the booze,
My gran's out playing Bingo,
　　But she was born to lose.

My brother's stripped his motorbike,
　　Although it's bound to rain,
My sister's playing Elton John,
　　Over and over again.

My baby sister's crying,
　　She doesn't want her bath,
I have to stand there dancing,
　　Trying to make her laugh.

What a dull old family,
　　What a dreary lot,
Sometimes I think that I'm
　　The only SUPERSTAR they've got!

Jane Webb

IN SCHOOL

The Lesson

Looking out of a sky-blue window,
A parting among the clouds,
Using a thunderbolt like a needle
Pointing out places on a map, which is real —

All the power of the galaxy
In a jar marked 'Universe'
That tadpoles used to swim in.

The way to make ant-people cower
By just blowing on the sea a bit,
Drowning the surrounding land . . .

A typical Geography lesson;
Even as far away as Jupiter
They study us, studying them.

Mhorag Forbes

*I was sitting talking to my mates when I remembered
a humanities lesson I had had a couple of years ago.
We had been taught about the solar system and that
ours was the only planet with life on it. Then, I would
have said 'Rubbish', if anyone had told me there was life,
other than us, in the Universe.*
*Now, slightly older and less sceptical, I often wonder
if there is life elsewhere. That's how the poem came
about. I just joined the two ideas together of my humanities lesson and our belief that somewhere out there,
someone is watching and studying us, while we make
feeble attempts to spot and study them.*
*The main reason for writing the poem was, I suppose,
to prove that anyone could write a 'futuristic' poem,
as well as using it as an outlet for my ideas. When a
poem like this is written no-one can say 'That's wrong'.
You just have to ask yourself whether it could happen
or is happening*

I am a Deemmun

Im a deemmun
I dont no how to spel
I allwaze deay-dreem
and teechuz pik on mi
cos I dont kno how to reed
I dont kair wot pepel sai
I dont nead to reed or ryte
I am not goeng to chooz it in the
therd yeers an
I dont nede it in my Jobb —
Soh thair!
Whot do I kare!

Julia Ignatiou

The Full Stop

I am a full stop.
I stop after every sentence!
(Well nearly every one because that was an exclamation mark.)

I will stop at the end of this line.
Did you know that without me there would be no sentences.
Instead they would just be carrying on in one long, very long,
so long, incomprehensible story.
(Get the idea? . . . . . . unlike this poem).

So you see I am important.
In fact so important I'm better than a comma.
They're useless compared to me.
Question, speech and exclamation marks are not as superior
                                                        as I.
For I am used as a first lesson in English:-
"Always finish a sentence with a FULL STOP."

I am also the easiest to write.
One dot is a full stop.
Speech marks are too high for me, I have vertigo.
Exclamation marks look too military.
"Yes Sergeant!!" (see what I mean?)

But my favourite is the tense end of a story.
It's a good way of finishing stories.
Look at this example.
Then the Martians landed . . . . . .

Edward Hickman

Never Ever Tell

He always had a good excuse
To stay away from games.
On the hottest days
He would stay fully-clothed.
He never came swimming.

I remember
One day our class —
Called to the medical room —
Asked to strip to the waist.
He pretended not to hear
His name called
Again and again.
With tears in his eyes,
He pulled his jumper over his head
And fumbled his buttons.
He stopped,
Walked over to the nurse
Whispered in her ear.
She pointed to the screen,
He stepped behind them and waited his turn.
When it came
He rushed from behind to the Doctor's office
Hoping none of us would see.

But we did.
And we couldn't understand
The fuss.
Lots of people have eczema.

Michael Lowe

First Day at the Nursery

The so-seemed castle had opened.
Amazed by all those unknown faces,
My stomach tightened, but had no tears.
I knew my Mum would go.
I saw Jenny, I felt gladness,
A power took us, made us all happy.

On the rocking horse I felt in charge of a
Cavalry, a leader, a master, I went fast,
I went faster.
Rolling in the mud I soon got muddy
Heavy and uncomfortable like weights, as the
mud dried.
A dreamy smell of mash and sausages, a
cradle and lullabies.

Karen Fitzgerald

Domestic Science

Sit down 1K
Burble, mumble, chatter
Sit down 1K
Burble, mumble, chatter
SIT DOWN 1K
God she shouts

Get your glass bowls out
Natter chatter natter chatter
Get your glass bowls out
Natter chatter natter chatter
GET YOUR GLASS BOWLS OUT
She could give you a headache

My god you're always talking
Natter chatter burble mumble
These kids don't stop
Natter grumble chatter natter
Will you STOP talking
Burble mumble natter chatter

Lisa Guthrie

A Close Shave

Another day is on the way
As the pips start ringing in my ear

Oh no! I forgot my letter about the other day
When I was away. Trouble!

She comes walking in the door
She gets closer to the drawer
She gets the register out
She starts to call the names
She gets closer and closer to my name
I'm going to be in trouble
I say yes!
She goes on!
She forgot, forgot, FORGOT!

David Bryant

Us Dreads

In a dis ya skool
us dreads rool.
Soul head dem saaf
mek us dreads laugh
dem no no how fe dress
but us dreads strickly de bess.
Gal dem cool an
control dem part ah de skool.
Mek us dreads feel sweet
each day ah de week.
Teachars all weird
mek saaf buoy scared
but us dread move together
an control de skool.
De music we play
nice up de day.
Rythdym just nice it
Teachar dem no like it.
When exam come
some dreads run
dem carn do dem tings.
In de enn teachar dem win.
Us dreads carn get na wok
we strickly brok
lose out in de enn
but us dreads still frienn.

Dave Martin

A Friend to Trust

Dragged into the bogs yet again,

She tells me to have a fag with her
So she can bribe me into listening
To her boring antics with her bloke.

I think of me own mates
As I drag on the fag and half listen to her
Droning on.

I try to change the subject
Because I have had to listen to the same old thing
Day in and day out.
It's a joke!

I suppose she needs someone to talk to
And I'm the only mug around

It's not that I don't like her,
It's just that she insists on
Talking about him and nothing else.
Before she met him we were always together
and we always had a laugh.

Sometimes I wonder why I bother with her.
She's still my mate but I regret getting
Her bloke to ask her out.
Anyway I don't care
I've got me other mates
To think about.

Jacqueline McNish

The Backslappers

What greater secrecy of love
than the cracked tiles of the
boys' room where faucets drip,
bored to tears with tales of
girls succumbing? Through the
smoke rings they gather, nodding
and jerking their heads as they
lie about the ease they had in
breaking down the barrier of
mother-tightened pant-elastic.
The most graphic, his laugh
caught short, his fag suspended,
recalls her eyes bulging as he
led her to the haven of a darkened
garage, bulbs smashed to the oily floor,
past the gleam of elbow-greased cars
reflecting her illease as he led
her to the teastained mattress
erected to the worship of debasing.
His doubts are chased away as
he fills his lungs, assured that
they both enjoyed it.
Another deals the cards on spittle
and in a reversal of sight sees
his hand calloused and yellowed with
tobacco running through her hair,
diverting knots, smells the stench
of beer covering her face, regurgitated
later behind someone's fence like the
words he tells them all.
He feels the slither of his lips
smearing her sister's lipstick,
inexperienced and unwilling to learn.
But as he deals a king he ignores
the memory of her after-fumble tears,
the way she grabbed up her clothes
and tripped as she ran.
Those sitting on sinks, in front of
various phone numbers, simply smile
and count their belt loads
of broken hymens, doubtless.

Jennifer Mitchell

54

CITY LIFE

View from the Window

Mathematical shapes creep in at the door,
Geometric squares stare up from the floor.
The ceiling is white — it used to be blue —
And the dope of this world is benzene-based glue.

An architect lives in a house on the green,
The windows are bay and the paintwork is clean,
But what he designed for my family
Was a garden of concrete with breeze-block for sky.

The stairways are signed by unknown hands,
The balconies filled with fields of tin-cans.
The view from the window's the view from the door,
And the view from the roof is the view from the floor.

Aeons ago a man thought he would try
To design a prison to scratch the sky;
The walls would be built of blood, sweat and toil
While the country around he aimed to despoil.

He employed the armies of death and decay,
Architects' strategies were put on display,
Dividers and callipers goose-stepped with pride
But the cartridge was paper, and the rules only slide.

Towering siege-weapons dismembered the view
As a mass of black spears serrated the blue.
Finally the tower of doom was complete
And remaining problems were solved by deceit.

He ushered us in, and was then called away;
Now the children of despair come here to play.

David Green

This poem was written after hearing a song which had eleven stresses to the line; after it had finished I began to juggle sentences with a similar rhythm in my head. As a result of this I found I had the couplet which eventually was to conclude the poem.

The theme has great significance for me: I live on an ageing council estate in the middle of Islington. The descriptions of it in the poem are honest ones.

The idea of the poem was to explore the divide between the architects and the people (amongst whom I class myself and nine tenths of the population). Linked with this is the theme of the subjugation of the masses through the use of force.

Colour Prejudice

Black boy meets white girl, they hold hands,
At this touch Cupid's arrow lands,
But arrow in the front, or in the back,
It doesn't matter, he's still black.
Her parents give the black a miss —
That, my friend, is Prejudice.

White boy meets black girl, holds her hand,
Visions of a promised land,
Takes her home to see his dad,
Surprise, surprise, his father's glad.
Her mum likes him as well, you know.
Very strange, even so.
This way round they're not dismissed —
Again, my friend, that's Prejudice.

Peter Williams

City Scene

All brown and speckled
it flew down into the tree next door.
I stood there watching it
picking at the small round red fruit
now turning brown as autumn drew on.
The tree stood there neglected and alone,
save for that small beady-black-eyed creature
flitting from one branch to another
eating the over-ripe and sour cherries.
A large blackbird, uninvited,
swooped down into the tree
and ate all the thrush's fruit.
The thrush left the tree.
It landed on the grass in front of me,
watching me,
head cocked on one side,
its eyes, black glass like marble,
staring at me.
Feeling sorry for it, I reached out and
opened the window.
The sun glinted on the glass
and blinded me
just for a second,
but when I looked out again
it was gone.
I walked out into the garden up the path,
my fingers
stroking the small brown pebble
which I had picked up from the doorstep.
My hand cracks the air,
the pebble crashing through the branches of the cherry tree,
in an instant, the blackbird was gone.

Michelle Mylonas

The Paraffin Man

One hour I have been waiting,
or an hour and a half, shivering
and freezing because there's no
paraffin in the house.
Here he comes at the top of the road
delivering paraffin to almost every door.
He gets the pans and fills them with
the thin blue liquid
and pours it in a big funnel
and it flows into the pans.
He sits down in the van
and waits for the other man
to finish drinking his hot tea,
with me waiting to sit down by the heat.

Sharon Clayton

South Side

Newspapers and crisp packets
Drunk men with dirty jackets
Old cars with tyres stripped
Rubbish heaps where junk's been tipped
On the South side of the Thames.

Dirty faces, wearing rags
Used matches and ends of fags
Smoke and dirt from old cars
Smashed bottles and cracked jars
On the South side of the Thames.

Old tunnels full of dirt
Old people watching, feelings hurt
Grey walls full of graffiti
Big kids strong and meaty
On the South side of the Thames.

Broken street-lamp lights the night
Two youths quarrel and have a fight
Rag and bone men on horses and carts
Smoke in the pubs and the sound of darts
On the South side of the Thames.

Brown leaves, shrivelled flowers in a window box
Old ladies with nylon coats, wishing they were fox
Terraced houses pushing out smoke
Kids drinking water, wishing it was Coke
On the South side of the Thames.

James Smith

This poem was written as a piece of homework. I was asked by my English teacher to write a poem entitled 'On the South Side of the Thames'. I later changed this title to 'South Side'. This meant I had a chance to put down on paper all the little things I have noticed walking through the streets of south London. I must say though, that in this poem I have only put down the bad things about south London. There are a lot of good things I can think about it. I might even go on to write a poem including the good things about south London. I will have to see whether I get round to it.

Hospital

The white walls, echoing, lonely corridors
seem unwelcoming for a caring place.
The staring nurses and patients,
The abrupt and brief talk with the lean
Lady behind reception, her glasses
distorting the reflections of the gathering
place.
A quick rush for the playing area, but
your mother's firm hand pressing on your
shoulder automatically suggesting no.
The sitting down on a hard red chair, still
warm, with the shape of the previous person
still embedded.
The harsh, 'Next one please,' that turns out
to be all right, for doctor with the
most warming smile says:
'And what's wrong with you then?'

Brian Geary

London Transport

Bloody London Transport!
Waitin' in the rain,
'Ere comes a 43,
An' another one again.
Been waitin' for a 172,
Been waitin' half an hour,
Been waitin' at this flagpost
All through this blasted shower.

An' as I stands 'ere at this sign of incompetence
With me nose turnin' red with cold,
As I stands 'ere at this flagpost
Me eyes do slowly close
An' I imagine all the buses
Comin' down the road in line — a 43
A 172, an 8 an' a 109 —
When all I want is a 172
To go and buy some peas.
Instead I 'ave to stand 'ere
Knockin' me knobbly knees
An' then I gets pneumonia
An' 'as to go to 'ospital
An' it's the ruddy government
That'as to pay the blasted bill
An' instead of wastin' money
On people who've been waitin' in the rain
When the people are goin' to have to wait in the rain again
Why don't they spend the money
On makin' a bus service Oh-so-grand
That when I wants to go somewhere
I've got every number at hand!

A 43 for Maggie's
A 172 for peas
An 8 for the butcher's shop
An' no more knockin' knees.
Ah maybe some day my dream will come true —
Oh look 'ere comes a 172 —
That'll do!

Nuala Moroney

Run Riot

A brethren throws a brick
an' a * bull get lick
A sister throws a stone
an' more bull come down.

*Babylon tek out dem riot shiel'
but dat nah stop dem from bleed
'Stop all this violence' a shout from de crowd,
but it was no use, the frustration grew loud.

Babylon a run but me don't know why.
Youthman a run but me still don't know why.
School children a run, but why?

'Dem a run fe dem life.
Man a fe hol' up him wife
dem a try to survive
fe stay alive.'

A white man chucks a rock
an' a shop window brok,
Black han' white han'
looting out de lan'.

looting, fighting against the
babylon
Trying to achieve a war dat
should be won.

'Fire,' shouted one man.
They had lighted a light blue van
Riot on de lan'
from those with the wicked han'.

Will de violence ever end,
and the heart aches ever mend?
Shall we have truth and right,
and stop the fuss an' fight?

Beverley Skyers

* *Two words meaning policeman/men.*

Daily Madness

He sips his tea
through printed lips,
but his rectangular eyes
won't leave that paper.
Each paragraph he reads
turns him more insane.

The creases in his wrinkled brow
are lines of inky black print,
His straight grey hair
falls in neat columns,
His hooked bony nose
is a photo of a diplomat.

His hard-set cheeks
Head an unimportant advert,
His old wrinkled forehead
is the news headlines.
The centre pages are unobtainable;
What would be found inside?

Justin Walinete

Winter in the City

The snow spreads her long white coat
across the fields and houses.

Then comes the frost,
who paints his grey-silverish
colours on the windows.

Then comes the wind,
who blows down all the loose tiles.

Next is the hail, who tap-dances
over everything, and jogs
down all the lanes,
and rattles on the windows of the buses.

Leroy Taylor

The Production Line

Nick paints the outside
Stan paints the inside
They do it all through the day
Tom does the nuts up
Bill does the bolts up
They always do it that way
Alf puts the wheels on
Bert puts the tyres on
They fix 'em so they're O.K.
Ted puts the engine
Arthur puts the boot in
But Fred's ill and he's not here today
Len puts the front seat in
George puts the back seat in
They fix 'em so they'll stay
Dan puts the lights on
Henry puts the bumpers on
Waiting for a tea break so they can get away
John puts the steering wheels in
Charlie puts the key in
And drives the car away
They can't stop long
Because as soon as that one's gone
There's another one on the way.

Bobby Pearce

Each Day

Seven a.m. by the clock. The bleakness of the street below
    and the grey lethargy of the morning
Force the sleepy eye shut again in weak despair, and hope,
    that in ten minutes or so, the scene will change.

Five a.m. by the sun. Streaming through the open window.
    Outside, the glittering world of varnished leaves and bright
        plumed birds instantly
    Captivates and draws away weariness, planting the will to
        work, to live.
    An invitation as warm and irresistible as the sunlight, calls
        to the sleeper in the bed.

Midday; coffee and sandwiches, greasy hair, split nails, foul
    language from cleaners in the canteen.
The prospect of going back to that office of piled-up
    garbage and slogging away at a sticky typewriter
    leers in front.

Scorching and uncontrollable, the sun's fury mounts, until at
    Midday it reaches its peak. Inside the white-washed villa the
        labourer takes his siesta, cool and comfortable
        after his bath, stretched out on his mattress.
    Next door, his wife and his children, his happiness, lie
        sleeping.

Harsh lights glare glassy-eyed onto the drugged atmosphere.
Evening, in the city of the leg-and-lipstick women.
Crude music with a synthetic throb heaves the air.

Pale pastel patterns paint the sky at the close of day.
Scent from the Tagore blossom and the incense for evening
           prayer
Combine to fill the air with quiet peace and restfulness.
Through the open window, past the veranda, the labourer
           and his wife follow the rites of their
Simple worship with small candles and their humble offering
           of flowers. As they pray the
Scarlet disc descends from darkening skies.

Muna Chakrabarti

You Never Took Me

I have six C.S.E.'s to be exact
I knew you wouldn't take me
and that's a fact.

When I had 'phoned for the job
I spoke very well
Though I was black
you just couldn't tell.

I went for the job
looking my best
I even passed your typing test.

When I had arrived for the job
I saw your surprise
and then you filled me
with all of your lies

You said to me you
wanted someone older.
A lump in my throat
I shrugged my shoulder.

You said "I'll hope you understand."
Then I arose and you shook my hand.

Yes; your reason I do understand!
You never took me and that's a fact.
You never took me because I'm Black.

Engley Stewart

THE FUTURE

Four Minutes

My friend, you have four minutes,
Four minutes of your long life.
My friend, what will you do —
Save your children and wife?

My friend, you have four minutes,
Tell me, what will you do?
It's your decision, yours to make,
Be careful you don't make a mistake.

Now, if we're generous, you have only three.
Come on, my friend, what will it be?
You can't afford to waste this time,
The life being taken isn't mine.

My friend, you're losing, you only have two.
I told you the future depends on you.
What do you mean, you didn't know?
I warned you, a whole two minutes ago.

Nobody told you four minutes was fun.
Come on, my friend, you only have one.
What are you doing? Running away?
Running with people? Don't believe what they say.

They're running for shelter, with thirty seconds to spare.
What are you saying, you weren't aware?
I told you a whole four minutes ago.
What do you mean, you didn't know?

Karen Roxburgh

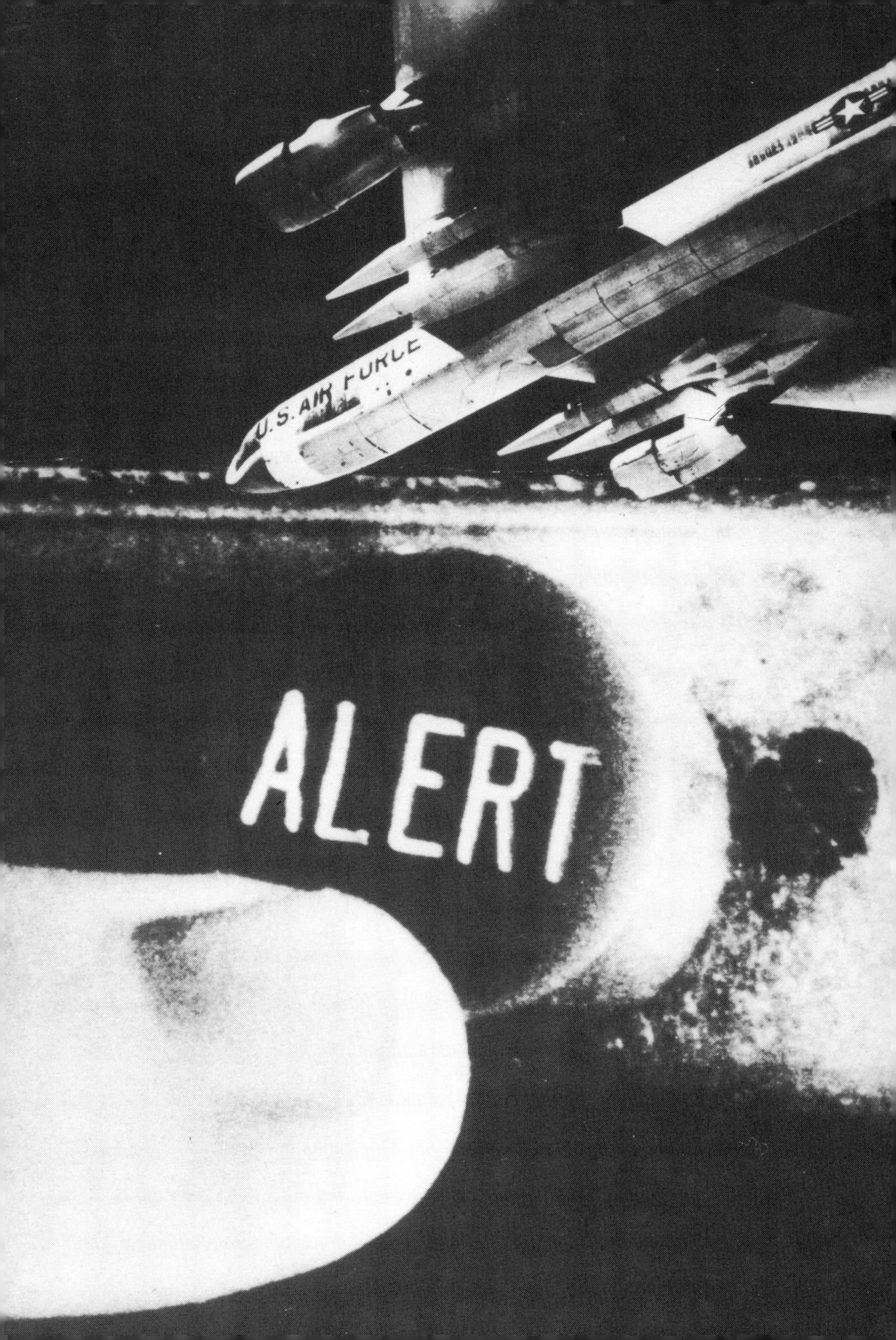
U.S. AIR FORCE
ALERT

The Ghost of Christmas Future

Sitting smugly on your little planet
You think you can change me.
You are so conceited that you're sure
That you can rearrange me.

But it is too late, you planned me
In an age that's brushed aside,
Now it is too late to change me
Even if you really tried.

You have struggled through the ages
To be lord of every kind.
Now you think you've won the battle.
I am here to change your mind.

I, the ultimate Cassandra,
Shall give warning to you all,
I shall let you see your future
As about the Earth you crawl.

You, however, won't believe me,
You'll be laughing in my face.
You will cry "God will protect us."
Proud, self-centred, human race.

In my mind you all will see
A little boy with golden hair.
He, indeed, will be the future,
Walking slowly to a snare.

Soon this child will be an orphan
In a country all alone
Wandering about a cornfield,
One huge garden of his own.

But this garden will be poison,
In this field no corn will grow.
It was shrivelled by that heat-flash,
Many, many moons ago.

Poison worse than deadly nightshade
In this garden's wicked kiss;
Horrors yet of radiation
Hidden in its empty bliss.

Soon the golden boy will vanish,
As all creatures surely must.
Gentle winds will try to heal him,
Weeping on that pile of dust.

He has gone, what God could save him?
Could not save the others, too.
If he did not save the others,
Why on earth should he save you?

Angela C. Payne

*I was glad that this poem was chosen for publication,
as nuclear warfare is a subject which I feel very strongly
about.
I had never before attempted writing protest poems, so
I decided to broach the most difficult subject first. This
could have proved disastrous, as I tend to ramble
blindly on about such subjects, but as it was, this
proved to be one of my better projects.
Poetry is an excellent sounding-board, in that you can
express your feelings on paper, and you can always
throw it away if you really don't like it. Emotions,
political views, large or small issues, it can even prove
personally helpful, as a way to gather your own
thoughts.
I was particularly aware of future possibilities at the
time of writing this poem, as I had to consider my
career and, indeed, a large part of my personal future.
I want to nurse when I leave school. I don't want to
have to treat radiation sickness. I also don't want to
have to think twice about having children, because their
future might not be worth having.*

Naturally

Daffodils stand like soldiers
with golden helmets,
bending together in the breeze,
whistling as they sway,
looking as if their
leaves curled round triggers,
firing pollen.

Suddenly the air is still,
the whistling stops.

Balding birds make fists of wings
to cough into,
as waterlilies drown.
Roses weep behind their veils
as purple skies
slowly smother picnic parties.
A mother drops the ladybird
that had greyed and powdered in her hand
and wraps her child
in a checkered cloth,
hugging her tight.
A dog, his hair falling behind him,
barks at the deathcloud,
while father scurries
to build a shelter
under a large oak tree
(with hearts engraved)
that bends its boughs
as if to pray.

Jennifer Mitchell

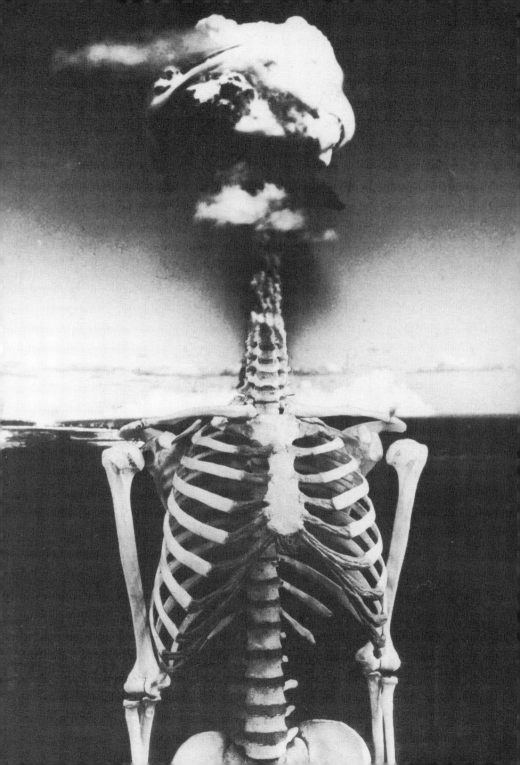

The Child

Smell fresh water while you can,
While still a creature free from man.
His influence doesn't reach you yet,
He regards you as an insignificant pet.
You're too ignorant to understand
The filth and plotting man has planned.

But that's a blessing; saved a bit from something sinister,
Though it means you're ill-prepared to meet with man —
                                        the monster.

Your thoughts are simple and straightforward,
So what if they say it's untoward?
But alas, you *do* have a narrow view,
Not enough scope to realise what they'll do to you.

For, contaminated you have been born,
There's but one restricted way for you to form;
You must, one day, become all they are,
Yes, those things you watch being wicked from afar.

The gradual change will happen every day,
You'll feel your attitudes start to sway.
You'll feel it happen, but you'll be helpless, you know,
Your old emotions are things you'll be frightened to show.

For every innocent freedom is a preventative law,
They point at you, saying — immature!

When your programming's over, and by their ugly standards
                                        you're near correct,
They throw you in alone among their sect.
No matter that you try to fight the change away,
You'll wake up and belong with them one day.

So, stay on the beach. Go on playing with your sand.
You don't appreciate the anguish that's at hand.
Take advantage while you can still be wild,
Before they change your happy state; a child.

David Upshall

*The idea for the poem was sparked off while I was
listening to a record. The lyrics immediately made me
think of a child, by the sea, playing with sand on the
beach. At the same time I remembered how I'd once
been like that myself; yet now I'm so different. I could
see that one day I'd be like all the adults around me.
I'm gradually losing all my innocence all the time —
and there's nothing I can do to prevent it.*

*Unfortunately as we grow, we gain the capability to
destroy — only a child with its total innocence lacks
the ability to do this. But we were all like that once!
When I was ten, I didn't want to get any older, but I
was determined that I'd always understand the feelings
of a child when I grew up. I've not even finished growing up yet, and already I cannot identify with a ten
year old and deep down I know that ultimately I'll be
like all the adults who sometimes don't understand me
now. I'll lose contact as I get older and become something different.*

*And, ironically, it's only when you're older and you
have lost your innocence that you can look back and
see how wonderful it was to be unaware of what the
future held, and you could play uninhibitedly, with no
responsibilities. Be careful: that's The Child..*

White Flakes

Will there ever be the final Solitude?
that sound that numbs our ears, rings out
with bursts of light,
the sky is pink with the glowing death,
or is it our blood-drowned eyes
so weak, they sleep in our sockets
some dead.
The man on the wooden box, told us
we would survive;
we listened to this last stranger in
pathetic obedience.

The hours are long gone,
the flash was a blood stain
that dripped for a moment;
and now it's beginning to snow
white flakes,
but it burns.

Anthony King

'White Flakes' didn't 'come to me in the night',
unfortunately. I sat in the classroom listening to
myself, over and over again in my mind, throwing up
words and writing them down.
It was like working on a sculpture — from something
rough and basic, I tried to create something distinct.
My main task was to try and veer off of the usual road
(as I've been frequently reminded by friends, of the
lack of originality of writing about nuclear war etc.).
I tried to combine the inevitable impact of the bomb,
with the suffering that might remain, the more physical
view of an exploded bomb, but most of all the pathetic misunderstanding of nuclear war. I tried to do this
by bringing the mood of the poem down after the
climax — I hoped to present the uselessness of it all.

When will be the Day

When will be the day
that on the tower
of the Parliament
the Red Flag
will play between the winds
with the British one.

When will be the day
that the students from every school
will make a festival
based in love and friendship
and we among these
and the teachers
and the schoolkeepers
and the black women
who work in the kitchen.

When will be the day
that poets will come to me
running
with their arms open
telling me
"Oye loco", we wrote the same things!

When will be the day
that the worker from the factories
(after their work)
with a sailor
with the shoe cleaner,
and my brother
will go out
to the pub
and drink the best beer
together.

When will be the day
that the beautiful girl
who lives in the flat on top of mine
will look at me, not as a stranger
not superior, because
I speak English with a funny accent
or because
she has blonde hair and blue eyes
and I
I have black curly hair
and dark brown eyes.
And I could kiss her lips
without worrying about her mam
watching from the window
and telling her
"Be careful love, these foreigners
are all the same".

When will be the day
that my companera
me and you
your sons and mine
will play football
and if someone comes
he'll play too
and the 2B bus will stop
and all the passengers
will come out and play football
and the conductor
and the bus driver
and after that everyone
will come to my house
or to yours
or to the old lady's
who was resting next to the door.

For that day
many Carlos will have
to give their blood
and many Mariellas
will have to give theirs
and once
a Carlos and a Mariella
will see that
will drink that best beer
at that pub!
will see that red flag.
on the tower of the parliament!
will sing in that festival!
will kiss that girl!
will play that football match!
will go to the old lady's house!
they will live!!!

Juan Carlos Bello

I came to England from Chile as a result of a fascist coup in 1973 in which my father was killed, along with many others, in the Santiago football stadium.

I remember the day I wrote this. I had been to two disappointing meetings in London about the possibility of a strike in Chile. I hoped the strike would be that day, but at the meetings I learned it was further off than that, so I thought — when will be the day? I realise it won't come just by hoping; many will have to give their blood, as I say in the poem, and fight, to bring that day.

I didn't write about Chile directly in the poem. I wanted the readers to relate the poem to themselves, so I set it in England. It's clear enough.

I also write poems in Spanish, but I don't translate them because they are then not the same poems, and also I can't play with words in English as I can in Spanish.

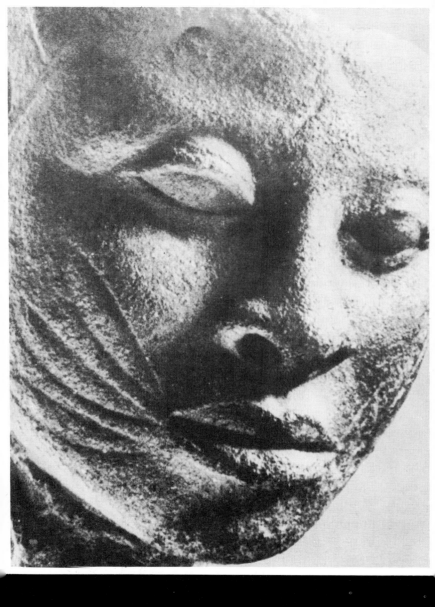

IMAGININGS

The River

Beneath the great concrete maze of the human race,
where the hustle and bustle of every day life
allows not for imaginings
There flows the river.

In the darkness there
It flows,
Through the musty time-worn caverns
on its way to nowhere,
mile after dank mile,
incessantly,
tirelessly,
on, on, on it travels.

It does not glisten,
it needs no sun to brighten its black waters.
On it goes,
Never stopping,
On forever,
Through eternity and beyond.

Beneath the great concrete maze of the human race,
where the hustle and bustle of every day life
allows not for imaginings.

Lynda Elieve

Stories of Old

Where are the witches who sailed above the clouds on
                                    Halloween night?
Where did they go? Why did they take flight?
And where are the dragons, once said to have gold
Long ago, in the stories of old?

Where are the elves, bright-eyed and watchful,
Who protected their lands from the ogres so terrible?
Where are the dwarves, the great wielders of stone,
Who sat in great halls underground, all alone?

Where are the zombies who drank human blood?
Where are the trolls, all smeared with mud?
Where are the werewolves who used to croon
From hilltops at night under the full moon?

The witches are now only legends,
And dragons and werewolves only live in tales.
Elves and dwarves now only wield poems,
But vampires can *still* chill our blood and our bones!

Nancy George

I am the Sea

Here in my depths are countless wonders
Coming to the surface in a bubble of air.
Strange aquatic beings, dancing
In the broken rays of the sun.

I am the sea: I am the beholder.

My eye is green and sees all those who wander alone.
My temper is rough and vengeance grave. Murky caverns
                                        entomb
Those who would dominate me.

I am the sea: I am true power.

When winds subside my wretched waves fade
To nothing but a ripple.
My roar, the roar of a lion, diminishes
To no more than the purring of a kitten.
My green waters become strangely inviting.

I am the sea: I am wild and unpredictable.

I keep a vault; a part of myself
Where secrets are locked away far from prying eyes,
Where disappearances become normality.
A triangle whose depths are unexplored and whose fruits
                                        are forbidden
To those who live in search of them.

I am the sea: I am the possessor.

My swirling waters fly with white-peaked caps
And within myself live endless fantasies of dreams untold.
My sunsets are a multitude of feelings
Bound together with a purple twine.
My call is a lover's beckoning whisper.

I am the sea: I am the temptress.

My storms are such that every living being
Will shake for fear of its life.
And once you have drifted far enough into my realm
And the boundaries of my estate are out of sight,
The unmistakable shadow of my sharp-finned warriors
Will remain constantly with you.

I am the sea: I am the commander.

Jannette White

*The mention of waves has always fascinated me. I have
spent many hours alone on the cliffs at Broadstairs
just watching them rolling in and out. I find a strange
calmness in their actions and have found it easy to
think because of them.
I also, rather ironically, have a fear of free-flowing
water, especially the sea, probably because of its great
power.
While on holiday in Wales I visited a place called
Swallow Falls, half way up which was a beautiful, still,
clear pool. It was surfacing from this pool that gave
me the idea for the second and third lines in the poem.
You aren't looking into the pool at the sea-creatures
below, instead you are looking up past them and seeing
the sunshine broken up in the ripples of the water.*

MY
NE
CK
IS
LO
NG
My sinews
strong Fine
wood my trunk
is made with- No
arms, no toes
a bridge, no nose-
I may be a guitar-well
Who knows? I fret, though
I am played with. How can
it be, I have no eyes
yet I can C? How
is it that though
I am round I
can B flat?

Kevin Dickson

He's Going

He's going out of this world
    Maybe into another
No-one knows   No-one

    Cares
His basket empty
    As I imagine him

His big brown eyes looking
Down on the floor
    His head on the corner of his
Basket as he
    Scratches   Oh, why did
he die?

Elaine O'Donovan

This poem was written for a class magazine. The class was asked to write a poem on anything they liked. I wrote my poem about a child who has lost a mongrel dog and who remembers all the little things the dog did and wonders if there is a heaven for dogs. The reason why I chose this subject is a bit related to the fact that I have a black and white dog of my own and this is what I would most likely feel if he were to die. Of course I hope that he will not die because I love him very much. I have not written a lot of poetry but when I do write I like to write about everyday things and ordinary feelings.

Domestic Cat

Domestic Cat's contented eyes narrow to slits,
Dreaming on a tropical beach — bathing in a chosen pool
of sun?

No!
Waiting for the imminent dawning hour — the hour for
feeding,

Waiting,
Like a gun triggered for action: Bang!
He jumps suddenly —
With agile ease trots —
With carefree urgency runs.
He rubs twisting between my legs, tying himself in knots
round my feet,
He purrs, looking benevolently in anticipation at me.
Once his cupboard-love has won me over and his food is in
front of him,

He leaves me.
He gingerly dabs at the fleshy mass with an experimental
paw,
Quick temperature test with the tip of a contradictory
small pink tongue.
He eats with the delicate fury of a lion having procured its
kill.
Turns his head from side to side, finding the required
cutting edge,
Finishes with a lick of his chops.
Languidly he strolls back into the shadow,
He jumps to his shelf with the ease one climbs a stair.
Settled, he picks and pulls at the now-soiled pink-padded
paw.

Claws splayed —
Tongue flashing in, out —
Eyes concentrating,
His ears are alert as he is unaware.
With lavish sweeps of his head he switches his concentration
                              to his already snow-white belly,
The tiers of pure white fur peel back revealing baby-pink
                              flesh, held under his rasping tongue.
Ending with a careful scrutiny of his tail, he lulls back
Mellowed full,
He eases himself to comfort.
Removed momentarily from character he flumps onto his
                              side;
As an after-thought he carefully twists his upper half over,
                              to stare out of the window,
Like an old man moving his gaze to peer at someone over
                              his glasses,

Spread-eagled,
Limbs rigid in taut apathy —
Plays dead rabbit.

Hannah Mayall

Dreams

I stand in a parking lot
the sun shines,
my throat is parched
A red van with a pink rose
painted on the side
drives slowly up to me,
I step in
A fair-haired man with a stubbly beard
hands me a cup from a flask
cracks into it an egg
and with a wrinkled hand
draws up the transparent white
it is drugged I know
Don't! my conscience cries
But I drink
A fiendish grin spreads across his evil face
'You fool' he cries
'You fool'
His evil green eyes glint in the sun
My head spins as I listen to the echo
'You foooooooool!'
His eyes fall out and crack like glass on the floor
All that is left where his eyes were is EMPTINESS
The shining pieces of green eye
grow together to form a tortoise,
no, a turtle,
growing larger and larger
it opens its gigantic jaws
out of the door I dash
I run and run
I'm being chased
I don't dare look back . . .
I WAKE

Miriam Bindman

My poem is based on a real dream. I had been thinking about it for many days, and when one day in English my teacher told us to write a poem about a dream, I could immediately start to write.

Writing the poem was like describing the picture I had in my mind of the dream.

I can remember in my primary school when I was about 7, a teacher once made a film of everyday school life. One part that I was in showed me putting down my shirt while changing for P.E. When the film was finished the teacher showed it backwards, so it looked as if my hand was a vacuum cleaner and the shirt came up to my hand. This is what gave me the idea of the man drawing up the egg whites in the poem. The poem is more or less an accurate account of the dream, except for the egg white idea and the real dream was much longer.

I Dreamed

I dreamed I was
a new missile —
and powerful countries
used to point me to the cities
to kill innocent people.

I dreamed I was
an American soldier —
and monopolies sent me
to El Salvador
to squash the people's voice
and hopes.

I dreamed I was
a Policeman —
and I used to go around
looking for black people
to put them in prison
for doing nothing.

I dreamed I was
a factory owner —
and I used to get rich
by exploiting workers
and killing their families
and lives.

I dreamed I was
a schoolboy —
with all my ideas of change
and I met other young people
with the same ideas
and we changed the world
and we lived in a society
where we were never
oppressed or prisoner.

Juan Carlos Bello

I Am

I am a human being, a boy.
You may say I am a special compound which can
Think, can see . . . etc,
And a little bit different from cat, dog etc.
You may say I am a body with a soul
Which is living.
I have a special computer which requires no electricity.
It is in my skull.
It works all the time until night.
When it can't work, I can't work.
I have a special pump which pumps the blood all over
my body, and no electricity required.
It is in my left chest,
But it never stops or feels tired.
When it stops, I stop.
I have some other machines which require no electricity
And they never stop or feel tired.
But when they stop, I stop.
That's me.

However, I am still I!

Chun Po Man

Shades of Rosary

Like a pious crow she knelt;
Beads clicking out prayers.
Immaculate Conception inclined
a blue-draped head.
Thorns briared the Ransom's ears.
At her knees dangled
a silver agony,
blessing black thighs.

Concentration was intent
as outside December;
deep as the snow.
Ambition, the desire to be desireless,
irritated by Thomas' absence.
Bound by vows of no support,
each bead was fresh and direct
subduing memory.

The Lady's plaster piety
whispered hollow;
too far from the Assumption.
And bread and wine
refused interpretation.
Each flame's lustre
dropping with its wax
and penance too eager.
Lisieux sent word,
but worldly joints
continued to groan rebellion
against a young Bastille.

Denise King

If I remember rightly I think I wrote this poem at a time when I was drawn to Roman Catholicism. Having had no religious upbringing at all (in fact perhaps something of the opposite) I found the Church of Rome a very firm and rock-like insitiution of faith. Indeed there is something rather beautiful in Roman Catholicism, in a faintly heavy sense; all those candles and prayers, rosaries, lovely depictions of the Blessed Virgin Mary which hit you at a basic emotional level. However after a good bit of internal debate I came to much the same conclusion as Dr Johnson, i.e. 'I would be a Papist if I could . . . but an obstinate rationality prevents me.' Nevertheless this poem was not written as part of the 'great debate'. In fact it all sprang into being with the image of a kneeling nun looking something like (with a touch of poetic licence) a crow. For those not very knowledgable about Catholic things I should explain that Immaculate Conception, meaning in this case the Virgin Mary, is the belief that in her mother's womb the Blessed Virgin was filled with the holy spirit and was therefore born without original sin (she also remained completely sinless in thought or deed throughout her life). The Assumption is the belief that after her death the Virgin was received into heaven both body and soul as Jesus had been and as all the righteous will be after judgement by Christ. Lisieux is a reference to Saint Therese de Lisieux, a nun who once lost her faith but regained it. 'Thomas' absence' refers to the absence of Thomas during the first appearance of Christ to the disciples after his resurrection; Thomas refused to believe until the matter was proved to him; therefore this was the first doubt expressed at the central belief of the Resurrection.

Time

Tick tock; tick tock
Seconds going faster
Tick tock; tick tock
hours going slower
Minutes and seconds are all one in time

Time for playing, time for sleeping
time for going, time for weeping
time for singing, time for dancing
time for hops, jumps and people prancing
Minutes and seconds are all one in time

Time on clocks, time on watches
time on churches, time in cottages
time in flats, time on chains
time in cold streets, time in lanes
Minutes and seconds are all one in time

Time's a bouncing ball, a midnight rave-up
a person running, a breaking up

Someone rolling a silver dime
This movement has something to do with time
It's something you can't explain
like the tapping of feet in a deserted lane
the person's steps, a finger that beckons
are all in time by things call seconds

One last thing is called a minute
and it has sixty seconds in it
and sixty minutes make one hour
it takes a thousand of those to build a flower

This is what clocks always chime —
That minutes and seconds are all in Time

Cynthia Tobierre

Slant of Light

There is a certain slant of light
That forms before dawn.
The sun, burning with colours
Follows in dazzling array.
The silent darkness is swallowed
And the light of the burning sun
Fills the earth.

Skies, orange and misty,
Irregular in all forms
Are the scenery of the morning performance.

A movement — a mauve cloud passes
And the grey blue sky
Shows a patch of true daylight.
Flowers open their eyes.
They slowly open and unfold
Showing a hidden beauty
The orb of light has given them life and light.

The sun pushes as if with little effort
And appears in full glory —
Beginning, the start of a new life,
Brought screaming into a screaming world and

The star of the show
Passes over the fields and houses
Bringing forth a sustained life
And the ball of light
Glimmering with pride
Has given its full performance.
The first act is over.
The sun has now danced.

Rebecca Saunders

Letters and Colours

A — mind of tension red with pain
Rushing the danger of blood by a sharp kill
Pressure boiling inside

    Red the conscious-minded meddler whose guilt glows in vain
    the masterful invention whose blushes create pain

E — blue in the height moving up above
danger is the sign of the deep wild waves
silent are the cool puddles as the water takes its place

    Blue has most prides it blossoms so high yet again so low
    laughter with beings swimming and enjoying wet happiness

I — green are the feelings of my precious life
dressing is my nature the colour is my price
I — is the amount of lives for whom I spend my time

    Green is full of hatreds and brings scars to the heart
    but life is concerned and needed by its side

O — the black odour which leaves ashes in the ground
Round is this world damp as faces as darkness comes forth
A never-ending shadow roaming the night.

    Orange the sound of the sweet powerful singing in the room
    and of its sweet fruitfulness which blooms

U — yellow are the rays which lighten my life
It symbolises birth full of wonderful creations
Glamour is the youth coming nothing but forward
with its brightness

    Yellow the yelling of the corn in its rise
    the product which sparkles in my greedy mind
    no confidence is backing away all of man's strength
    and bringing it to Hell is another man's breath

    As for Indigo and Violet they rust all in vain
    time passes them quickly patience arises
    no interest is their nature no time is their game

Kathleen Bakie

200 Miles of Water

The morning was foggy.
Suddenly in the fog
A canoe was approaching
With two thin gentlemen
rowing it, you could
hear the flickering of the water.
When the oars were going forward
and backwards, all around you, you
could see thin long trees with no
leaves, but empty branches.

Golden leaves fluttering on the ground,
With no sign of human being,
treading on the soft golden leaves.
Nothing except the two men rowing their canoe
on the cold water and yellow, red
and golden leaves floating on the
surface of the water.

Blue and clear with the atmosphere
Full of freshening air and life.
The sun shining upon the trees and
glowing, the reflections of cliffs upon
the blue water, the sound of the
birds taking off with their little heads pointing straight.

And the grey cliffs dropping
over the water edge,
the red sky with blue in it
and the sun glittering upon the world
and keeping it warm.
The golden trees the shape of a
cliff, the stream running over
grey little stones and the fishes
hiding in their corners.
The night is over the darkness and there
is silence except for the two men rowing their canoe.

Regie Kumar

The Hewlett Packard 2000

RUN
SPRBRD

HERE IS THE POEM:

THE EVIL STAR
HELD A HOME AROUND RIDICULOUS PLANETS
AND SINGING NOVAE PASSED LOOSELY
FOR A HOLOGRAM . . . . . .

GOOD, ISN'T IT? DO YOU WANT ANOTHER ONE? YES.
HERE IS THE POEM:

THE INTERPLANETARY HOLOGRAM
GLIDED A PLANET AROUND LARGE NOVAE
BUT CRAZY DUSTBINS LOST SERIOUSLY
FOR A FLAVOURED CAT . . . . . .

GOOD, ISN'T IT? DO YOU WANT ANOTHER ONE? YES.
HERE IS THE POEM:

THE INTERPLANETARY NOVA
FLEW A DUSTBIN AT EVIL HOLOGRAMS
AND COLOURED DUSTBINS HELD SEARCHINGLY
THROUGH THE FLAVOURED PLANET . . . . . .

GOOD, ISN'T IT? DO YOU WANT ANOTHER ONE? YES.
HERE IS THE POEM:

THE INTERPLANETARY HOME
GLIDED A STARSHIP AT RIDICULOUS STARS
AND SINGING STARSHIPS LOST SEARCHINGLY
FOR THE FLAVOURED DUSTBIN . . . . . .

GOOD, ISN'T IT? DO YOU WANT ANOTHER ONE? NO.
PHILISTINES LIKE YOU OBVIOUSLY DO NOT
                                        APPRECIATE

PURE GENIUS!

DONE
SCR

List of Contributors

Kathleen Bakie 13 George Orwell
Juan Carlos Bello 16 Tulse Hill
Miriam Bindman 12 Parliament Hill
P.S. Blackman (Jnr.) 16 Quintin Kynaston
David Bryant 14 Roger Manwood
Danny Cerqueira 15 St. George's
Muna Chakrabarti 16 Burlington Danes
Sharon Clayton 13 Norwood
Joan Davidson 15 Vauxhall Manor
Kevin Dickson 11 Wandsworth
Kathleen Edmonds 14 Vauxhall Manor
Karen Fitzgerald 13 George Green's
Virginia Fletcher 14 Skinner's Company
Mhorag Forbes 15 Haverstock
Juan Berganinos Fuentes 15 Pimlico
Brian Geary 15 North Westminster
Nancy George 12 Greycoat Hospital
David Green 17 William Ellis
Lisa Guthrie 11 George Green's
Edward Hickman 17 Battersea County
Julie Ignatiou 13 George Orwell
Lynda Ilieve 15 George Orwell
Anthony King 16 Tulse Hill
Denise King 17 Waverley
Regie Kumar 14 Wandsworth
Michael Lowe 14 Daneford
Chun Po Man 16 Battersea County
Dave Martin 16 Tulse Hill
Hannah Mayall 16 Hampstead
Jacqueline McNish 17 Walworth
Maureen Miles 15 Brondesbury & Kilburn *
Jennifer Mitchell 16 South Kilburn High *
Martin Murphy 18 St. Joseph's
Nuala Moroney 13 Mount Carmel
Elaine O'Donovan 13 La Sainte Union
Angela C. Payne 15 St. Martin's-in-the-Fields
Bobby Pearce 14 Abbey Wood
Sonia Pearce 15 Pimlico
Delia Perez 13 Pimlico
Andrew Richmond 15 Wandsworth
Karen Roxburgh 15 Norwood
Rebecca Saunders 13 Pimlico
Jeanette Sharp 13 Vauxhall Manor
Beverley Skyers 15 Kidbrooke
James Smith 14 Scott Lidgett
Engley Stewart 16 Kennington
Leroy Taylor 15 Southfields
Katerina Theoharous 13 George Orwell
Cynthia Tobierre 14 Southfields
Ruth Tuschling 16 Burlington Danes
David Upshal 15 Malory
Demetroulla Vassili 12 George Orwell
Sonia Vigo 13 Ladbroke
Justin Walinete 13 Wandsworth
Jane Webb 12 St. Michael's
Janette White 14 Haggerston
Peter Williams 15 Acland Burghley

Photographs

p 9	Keith Hawkins
p 12	Keith Hawkins
p 16	Michael Simons
p 22	Eddie Gleeson
p 27	Dave Hampshire
p 29	Richard and Sally Greenhill
p 31	Richard and Sally Greenhill
p 35	Richard and Sally Greenhill
p 38	Mike Abrahams (Network)
p 41	Dave Hampshire
p 43	Keith Hawkins
p 44	Mike Abrahams (Network)
p 47	Keith Hawkins
p 48&49	Keith Hawkins
p 51	Dave Hampshire
p 52	Keith Hawkins
p 55	Richard and Sally Greenhill (Carnival Against the Nazis, Victoria Park)
p 57	Jenny Matthews
p 59	Richard and Sally Greenhill
p 61	Richard and Sally Greenhill
p 63	Richard and Sally Greenhill
p 67	John Sturrock (Network) (Brixton, April 1981)
p 71	Dave Hampshire
p 74	Laurie Sprarham (Network) (Fenner Brockway at a CND rally)
p 77	Peter Kennard
p 81	Peter Kennard
p 84	Chris Davies (Network)

* Brent (Our Competition poster went beyond
the boundaries of ILEA, and these two poems,
although not eligible to be prizewinners, were
thought too good to leave out of the anthology.

111